Enjoy! from your friends at Avery-Hess - Lake Ridge

VIRGINIA
A PICTORIAL SOUVENIR

CAROL M. HIGHSMITH AND TED LANDPHAIR

VIRGINIA

A PICTORIAL SOUVENIR

CRESCENT BOOKS
NEW YORK

THE AUTHORS GRATEFULLY ACKNOWLEDGE
THE SERVICES, ACCOMMODATIONS, AND SUPPORT PROVIDED BY
HILTON HOTELS CORPORATION
AND THE RICHMOND AIRPORT HILTON
IN CONNECTION WITH THE COMPLETION OF THIS BOOK.

Photographs copyright © 1997 by Carol M. Highsmith
Text copyright © 1998 by Random House Value Publishing, Inc.
All rights reserved under International and Pan-American
Copyright Conventions.

No part of this book may be reproduced or transmitted in any form
or by any means electronic or mechanical including photocopying, recording,
or by any information storage and retrieval system, without permission
in writing from the publisher.

This 1998 edition is published by Crescent Books®,
an imprint of Random House Value Publishing, Inc.,
201 East 50th Street, New York, NY 10022.

Crescent Books® and design are registered trademarks of
Random House Value Publishing, Inc.

Random House
New York • Toronto • London • Sydney • Auckland
http://www.randomhouse.com/

Printed and bound in China

Library of Congress Cataloging-in-Publication Data
Highsmith, Carol M., 1946–
Virginia / Carol M. Highsmith and Ted Landphair.
p. cm. — (A pictorial souvenir)
ISBN 0-517-18758-2
1. Virginia—Tours. 2. Virginia—Pictorial works.
3. Virginia—Description and travel.
I. Landphair, Ted, 1942– . II. Title.
III. Series: Highsmith, Carol M., 1946– Pictorial souvenir.
F224.3.H54 1998
917.5504´43—dc21   97–18035
CIP

8 7 6 5 4 3 2

Project Editor: Donna Lee Lurker
Designed by Robert L. Wiser, Archetype Press, Inc., Washington

PAGES 2–3: Three months after the surrender of Fort Sumter, Federal and Confederate forces met on a battlefield for the first time near Bull Run, an obscure creek in Northern Virginia. Contrary to rebel expectations, the humiliating Union defeat hardened President Lincoln's resolve to fight on.

FOREWORD

"Virginia Is for Lovers" is the state's much copied tourist slogan. And it is certainly a destination to where lovers of history converge. For no other state in the United States has been the center of more major events or the home of more key figures in the country's illustrious past. Virginians still speak proudly of "ffvs"—or a First Family of Virginia, a title accorded to families who trace their lineage to early English settlement. It is a state that reveres its great patriots and presidents, and the heroism of its soldiers—more than half of all Civil War battles were fought in Virginia. To this day the name of its greatest son, Thomas Jefferson, resounds throughout the state, as do the names and deeds of other legendary Virginians—Pocahontas, John Smith, George Washington, James Madison, James Monroe, Woodrow Wilson (and three other, less-remembered presidents, W. H. Harrison, John Tyler, and Zachary Taylor), Patrick Henry, Robert E. Lee, J.E.B. Stuart, and Stonewall Jackson.

Virginians took prominent roles in the creation of this nation. It was in Richmond that Patrick Henry, at the Second Virginia Convention in 1775, stirred the delegates to revolution against Great Britain with his cry of "Give me liberty, or give me death!" It was George Washington who was elected the new republic's first president in 1789. Virginia also relinquished the title to a small piece of land along the Potomac River that became the new national capital, Washington, D.C. Jefferson was elected president in 1800, to be followed by two trusted friends and fellow Virginians, Madison and Monroe.

It was a Virginian as well, Edmund Ruffin, on April 12, 1861, who fired the first shot that led to the capture of Fort Sumter and the beginning of the civil war that almost destroyed this nation. Richmond became the capital of the Confederate States of America and Robert E. Lee, already in command of Virginia troops, was named commander-in-chief of Rebel forces. As the Confederate state nearest to Washington, Virginia became the bloody locus of much of the war, beginning with the first Battle of Bull Run, and ending with Lee's surrender at Appomattox on April 9, 1865.

The state's most popular historic attraction is Colonial Williamsburg. Williamsburg was the capital of England's oldest and largest American colony. Colonial Williamsburg is a re-creation of a colonial village containing eighty-eight original structures, fifty reconstructions and forty exhibition buildings.

Even with this preoccupation on all things historic, Virginia, however, defies stereotyping. In this single state, one can leave the glistening strand of Virginia Beach for bustling fishing coves, indolent Tidewater marshes, cotton and tobacco fields, apple orchards, plantation homes, reborn colonial villages, explorers' outposts, wayside taverns, giant clothing and cigarette factories, unfettered suburban developments, an array of amazing caverns, the remnants of epic battlefields, and the parallel spines of mountains stretching four hundred miles from Maryland to Tennessee. No one metropolis dominates the state. That's all the better for enjoying the easygoing charms of Richmond, Norfolk, Roanoke, Danville, and other popular locales. Each extols new, vibrant architecture and public art, clubs and amusement parks, convention centers, and sporting venues, while holding tight to an illustrious past.

OVERLEAF: Virginia's restful Eastern Shore—a collection of barrier islands and a piece of a peninsula that includes parts of Delaware and Maryland—is a sailor's and sportsman's Eden. There, America's oldest continuous court records, in Eastville—also site of an old debtors' prison—date to 1632. More than 260 species of birds, and the famous Chincoteague wild ponies, inhabit Assateague Island's wildlife refuge.

Virginia Beach has grown into a sprawling seaside resort—the largest city in the state—but there are still plenty of remote paths and dunes (above). On Cape Henry, Jamestown colonists first touched the shore of the New World in 1607, thirteen years before the Pilgrims landed on Plymouth Rock. Nearby (right), at the point where the Chesapeake Bay spills into the Atlantic Ocean, stand the old, brick Cape Henry Lighthouse, built in 1791—the oldest government-built lighthouse in America and the city's official symbol today—and a newer lighthouse, built in 1879, that still guides ships along the coast. It was off Cape Henry that the French fleet, commanded by Admiral Count de Grasse, stopped the British Fleet during the American Revolution.

Todd Lindbergh was painting billboards in 1987 when the owner of an auto-repair shop asked him to create something unusual on the side of his building. He drew an oversized spark plug. Since then, he and his brother Eric—both high-school dropouts with no artistic training—have painted dozens of murals in the Virginia Beach area, including this underwater scene (left) on a wall of the Sunsations T-shirt shop on Atlantic Avenue. They sign their work "Talent," shorthand for "Todd Alan Lindbergh Enterprises." Up Atlantic Avenue at Thirty-first Street are eminently climbable beach balls—one of the city's many beach-theme public-art displays (above).

11

Nolfolk's waterfront is replete with attractions, including Nauticus, the hands-on National Maritime Center; the Waterside Festival Marketplace; and the U.S. Naval Base (opposite), the largest naval installation in the world. "Pavilions" were originally meeting places of desert travelers and Byzantine traders. At Virginia Beach's Pavilion—its convention center (left)—groups of several hundred or several thousand convene, display products, and attend performances. To the northwest in Hampton Roads, the Hampton Coliseum (above) is the site of an annual jazz festival that has featured many star performers. Here, the term "roads" refers not to a series of highways, but to a shipping channel at the mouth of five rivers, including the James and the Elizabeth.

At Jamestown Settlement, where America's colonial history began, three tall-masted ships—replicas of the three English ships that sailed to Virginia in 1607—lie at anchor in the James River. Aboard one, the Susan Constant (opposite), costumed interpreters guide visitors through the intricacies of seventeenth-century shipboard life. A reconstructed primitive church (above) is one of several buildings inside James Fort at the settlement. In the woods beyond the fort is a Powhatan Indian village, constructed from firsthand descriptions from English settlers. The settlement also offers indoor galleries, in which original artifacts and other exhibits covering the colonists' first hundred years are displayed. Jamestown Settlement and the Yorktown Victory Center at nearby Yorktown— both within twenty minutes of Colonial Williamsburg in Virginia's Historic Triangle—are operated by a foundation that is an educational arm of the Commonwealth of Virginia.

Statues of Pocahantas (above) and Captain John Smith (opposite) can be found at Jamestown Island, part of the National Park Service's Colonial National Historical Park. Pocahantas, the daughter of a chief of thirty coastal tribes, befriended English colonists, saved Smith from death at the hands of the Indians, married settler John Rolfe, and traveled with Rolfe to England to recruit new colonists. She has been lionized in poems, songs, and a hit children's movie of the 1990s. Smith, leader of the Virginia Company colony, recorded thorough descriptions of Indian culture. Down the Colonial Parkway, more than one hundred re-created eighteenth-century gardens (overleaf) are spread over Colonial Williamsburg's 173 acres. Archaeological excavations conducted on many sites revealed the remains of walkways, brick walls, and fence lines, which helped to determine the shape, size, and structure of gardens and outbuildings.

Most of Colonial Williamsburg's gardens (right) were planted from the 1930s through the 1950s in the refined Colonial Revival style, reflecting a nostalgic vision of the nation's colonial past. Through "landscape archaeology," the park's nonprofit foundation is gradually reworking its gardens to represent a more historically plausible— and less manicured— setting. The Governor's Palace (opposite) is one of the architectural attractions at Colonial Williamsburg. In 1699, after nearly one hundred years of battling famine, fire, and Indians, the leaders of the Virginia colony abandoned Jamestown for a new capital, named for the reigning King, William of Orange. Thanks to substantial bequests from John D. Rockefeller Jr., the Historic Williamsburg Foundation began preserving— and later restoring— the old colonial capital in the 1920s.

The tranquility of the Town of York, a bustling colonial tobacco port, was shattered in 1781 when American and French forces defeated British troops in the Revolutionary War's decisive battle. At the Yorktown Victory Center's recreated colonial army encampment, costumed characters (above) fire cannons to the delight of most observers. Up the James River, Shirley (right)—Virginia's oldest plantation—was founded six years after settlers arrived in Jamestown. The mansion, whose pineapple roof decoration was the colonial symbol of hospitality, was a supply center for the Continental Army and survived the Peninsula Campaign during the Civil War. Anne Hill Carter, wife of "Light-Horse Harry" Lee and mother of Robert E. Lee, was born there. Shirley Plantation is still a working eight-hundred-acre farm.

Virginia's 1785 state capitol (left) in Richmond, modeled after a Roman temple in Nimes, France, was the first public building in the New World built in the Classical Revival architectural style. Although it served as the Confederate capitol, the building was spared during the climactic burning of Richmond. On April 27, 1870, a crowd squeezed into its Supreme Court of Appeals chamber, collapsing the floor; sixty-two people died. President Jefferson Davis's photo (above) hangs in the parlor of Richmond's White House of the Confederacy, part of the Museum of the Confederacy. Founded in 1896, the museum maintains more than 80,000 artifacts, decorative items, books, and documents.

Richmond notables have lived on Monument Avenue—considered by some "America's most beautiful boulevard"—since city engineer C.P.E. Burgwyn laid it out in 1889. Monuments honor Confederate heroes Robert E. Lee, Stonewall Jackson, J.E.B. Stuart, Matthew Fontaine Maury, and Jefferson Davis. The statue of Jackson (above), shown ramrod-straight in the saddle at the Battle of Bull Run, was designed by F. William Sievers and unveiled in 1919. On another monument (opposite), created by Edward Valentine and unveiled in 1907, Confederate President Davis strikes an oratorical pose. The statue's thirteen Doric columns represent the eleven states that seceded and two (Missouri and Kentucky) that sent delegates to the Confederate Congress but were prevented from departing the Union. Atop a column stands the bronze Vindicatrix, *representing the spirit of the South but informally called "Miss Confederacy."*

The slogan of Danville, the principal city in Southside Virginia, is "Pick a Victorian flower." Architecturally, there are plenty to choose from on Millionaires' Row, one of the pre-eminent collections of Victorian and Edwardian architecture in the South. Most of its homes were built for wealthy tobacco merchants and the entrepreneurs who formed the Riverside Cotton Mills—the future Dan River textile company. Among the latter was John Harrell Schoolfield, who had his fellow founder, contractor Thomas B. Fitzgerald, construct a High-Victorian Italianate mansion (above) on Main Street. Down the street, the Queen Anne "Wedding Cake House" (left) was completed as a wedding gift in 1903 for Barnes and Mary Penn. The lavishly decorated mansion is now a bed-and-breakfast inn.

Tobacco was king in Southside Virginia—though today vineyards (opposite) are increasingly important throughout the Commonwealth. Danville warehouses (above) once brimmed with activity. Indeed, Danville was founded as a tobacco inspection center forty years before it was incorporated in 1833, and thrived long after many other communities in the Old Confederacy suffered economic depressions. Bright Leaf tobacco was developed nearby, and the "Danville system" of auctioning entire lots of tobacco was introduced in the city's warehouses. But this neighborhood in the "Last Capital of the Confederacy"— so named because Jefferson Davis, fleeing from Union forces, moved the government there in the final throes of the rebel nation—eventually declined into tawdriness before the city undertook a massive clean-up and revitalization in the 1990s.

The old stone structure (opposite), built in 1798, was the third Quaker meetinghouse built on this site in Lynchburg. Many Quakers, who opposed slavery, left Virginia for northern states. John Lynch, founder of the city, is buried in the Quaker cemetery behind the house. Randolph-Macon Woman's College (top left) was founded in 1890. Washington, D.C., architect William M. Poindexter employed the red brick, white trim, columns, and classical detailing borrowed from Queen Anne-style academic buildings in Great Britain. Robert E. Lee signed the Civil War articles of surrender in the parlor of the McLean House (bottom left) in Appomattox. The University of Virginia's signature landmark, the Rotunda (overleaf), is a half-scale interpretation of the Pantheon in Rome.

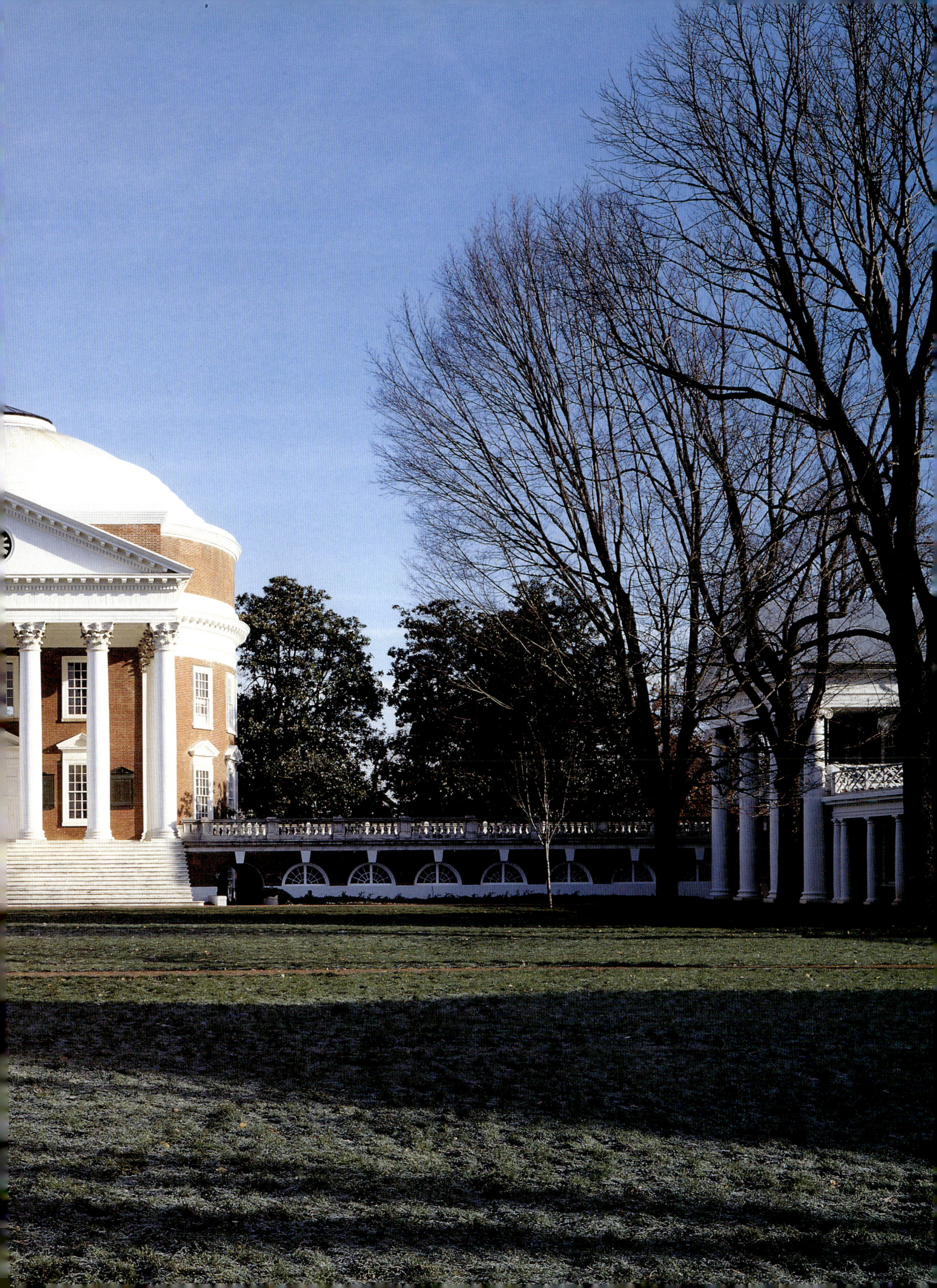

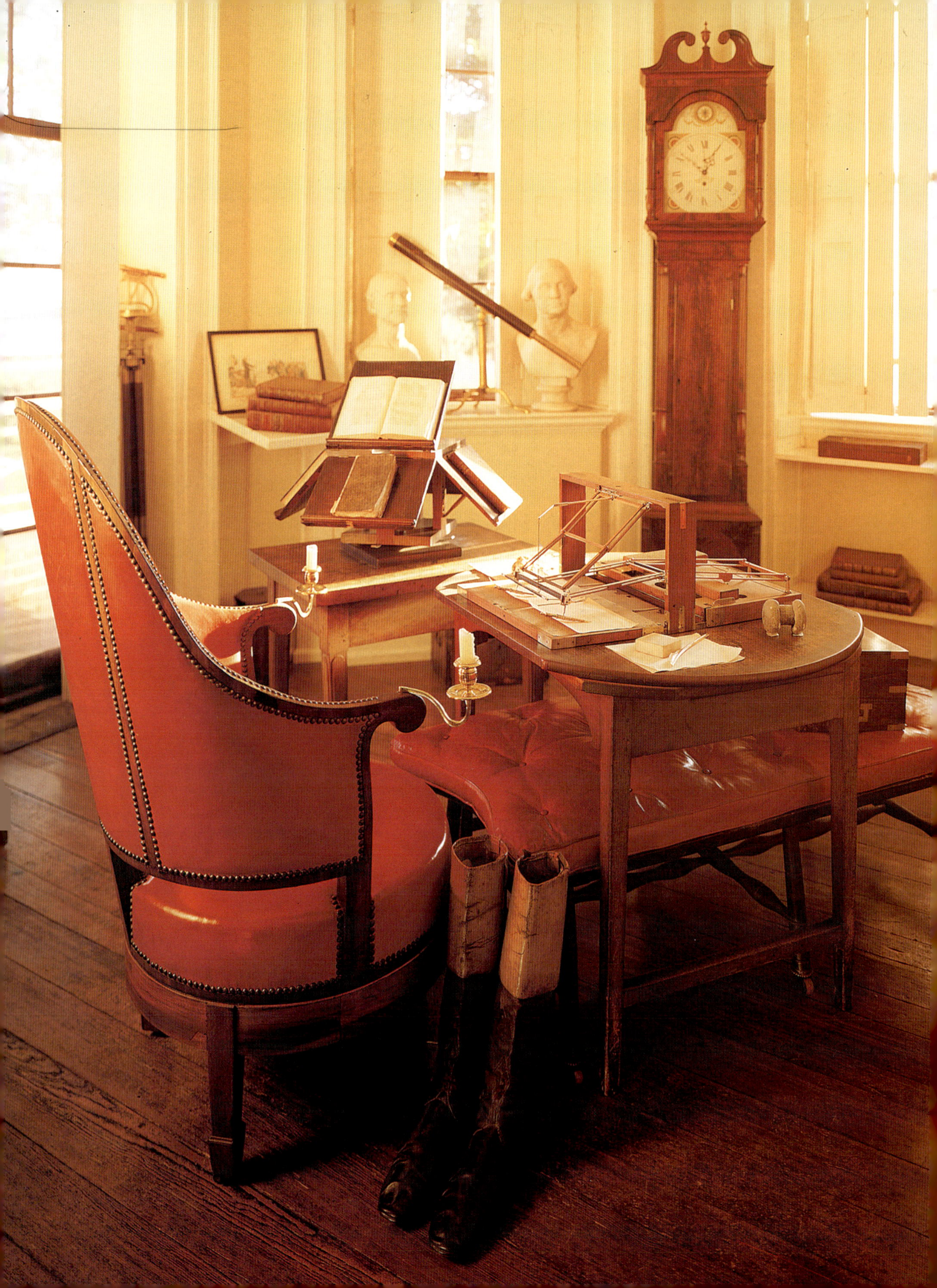

The Cabinet, or study (opposite), was the most private sanctum of Thomas Jefferson's home at Monticello (above), near Charlottesville. After spending five years in France, Jefferson completely redesigned his residence, adding the first dome ever seen in Virginia. Atop his study's rotating writing table he employed a "polygraph" copying machine to duplicate letters, of which he wrote more than twenty thousand during his lifetime. Jefferson reported that the polygraph worked by "copying with one pen while you write with the other." Monticello curator Susan R. Stein quotes him as confessing to John Adams: "From sunrise to one or two o'clock, and often from dinner to dark, I am drudging at the writing table. And all this to answer letters into which neither interest nor inclination on my part enters; and often from persons whose names I have never before heard."

George Washington's great-grandfather, John Washington, was one of the first settlers in Virginia's "Northern Neck," the area between the Rappahannock and Potomac Rivers. There, on the banks of the Potomac, John built a modest estate. His grandson Lawrence, George's father, named it "Mount Vernon," after British admiral Edward Vernon, with whom he had served. George acquired it in 1754 when he was twenty-two, and enlarged the mansion (above), which his father had constructed in 1735. Several original furnishings are still on display there. The nation's first president was an avid gardener. His plan for the estate called for three gardens, including an upper garden (right), full of vegetables, flowers, and trees. There were also a kitchen garden and a botanical array in which Washington experimented with seeds and plants not native to Virginia. All three are meticulously maintained to this day.

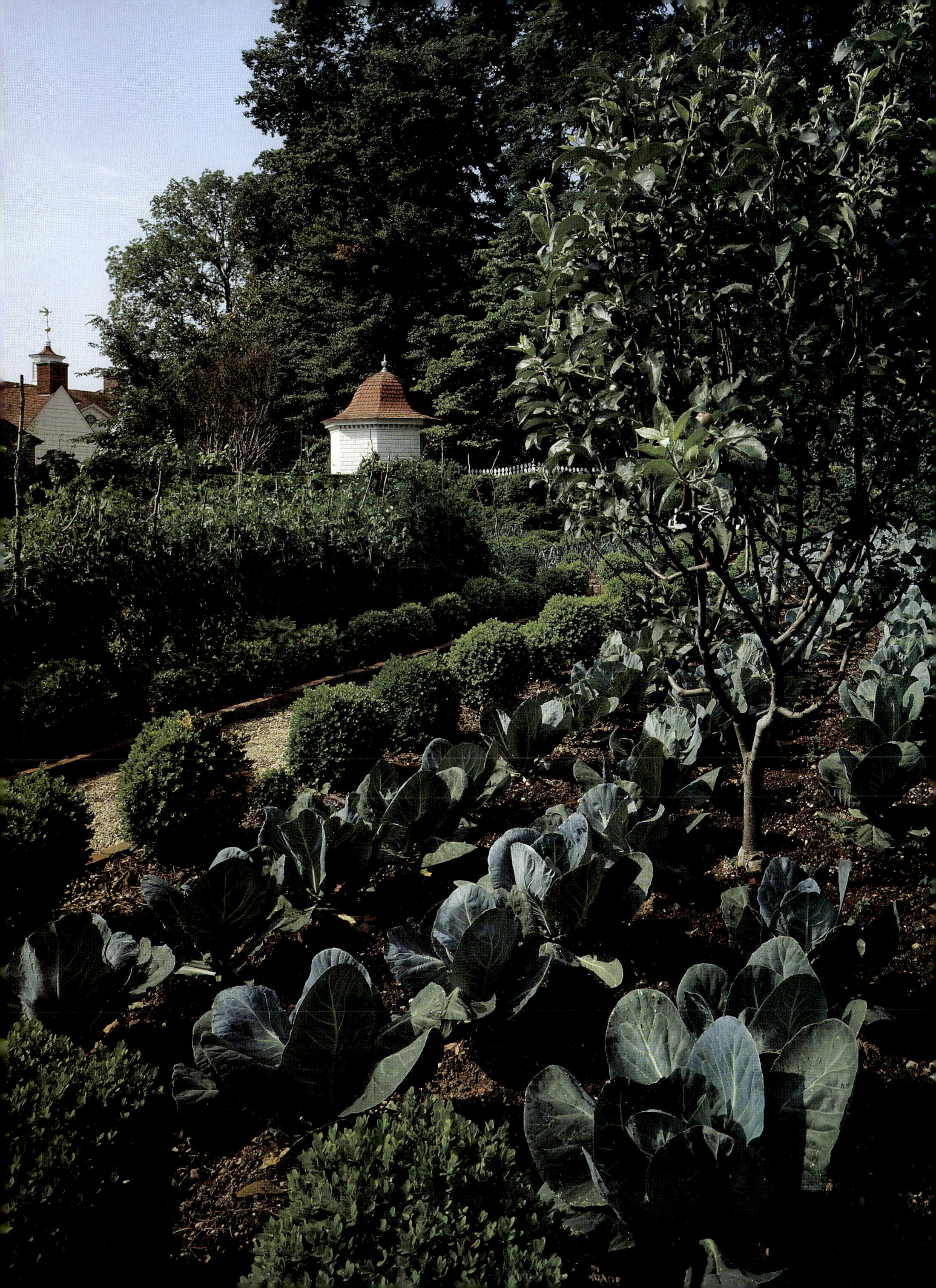

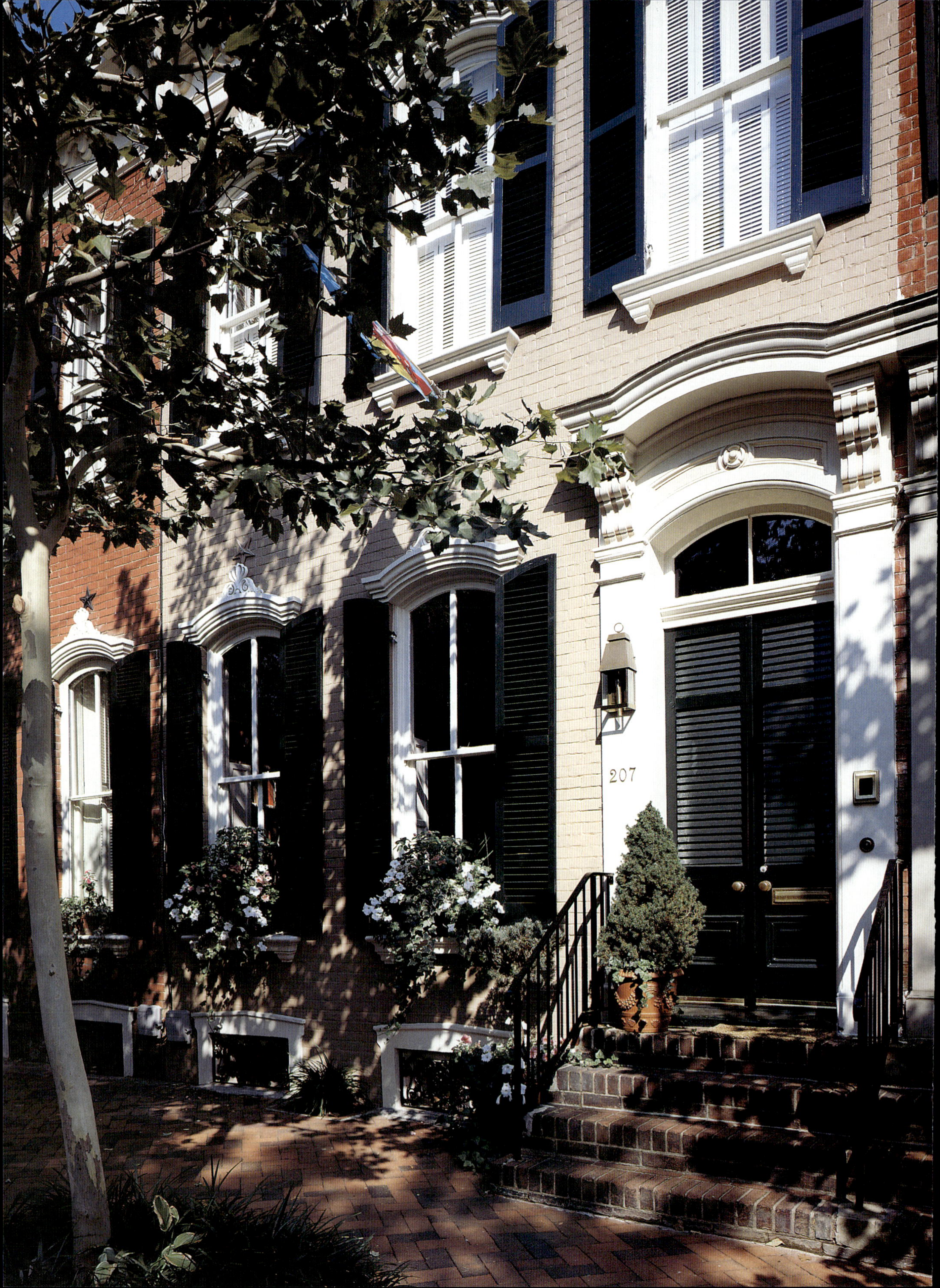
207

Alexandria was a thriving Potomac River tobacco port. George Washington—and Robert E. Lee generations later—walked the cobblestone streets and brick sidewalks that Washington had helped lay out. For almost five decades the city was part of the nation's capital, until it was retroceded to Virginia in 1846. Old Town Alexandria (opposite) has retained many eighteenth-century townhouses. Washington and Lee both worshipped at Christ Church (left), built in 1773. Here, Lee was offered command of Virginia forces in the Civil War. In Arlington, once a part of Alexandria, Union forces took control of Lee's estate and, to taunt the Confederates, built a cemetery (overleaf) for Union dead there. More than two hundred thousand military personnel and their dependents are now interred there.

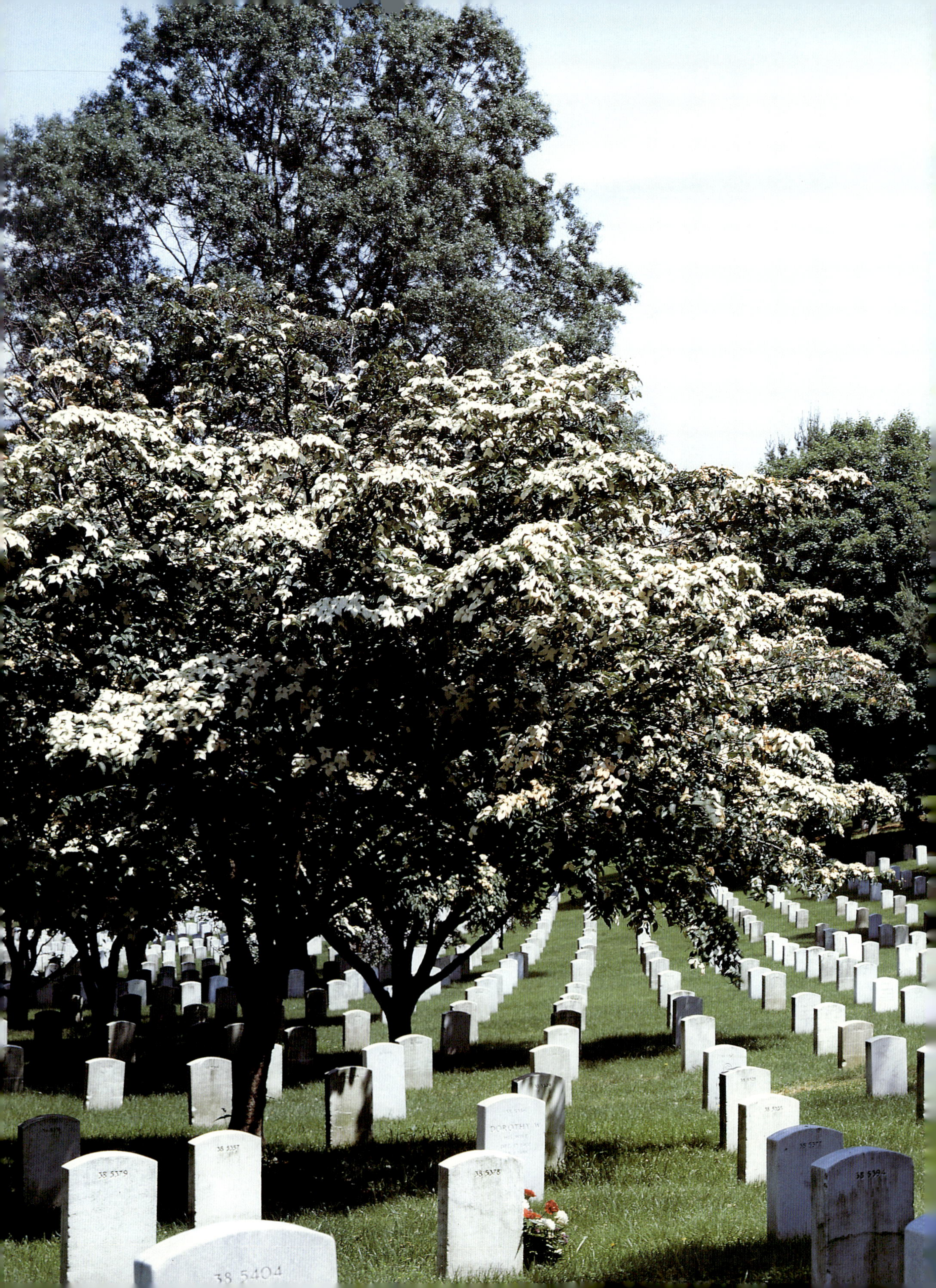
38 5404

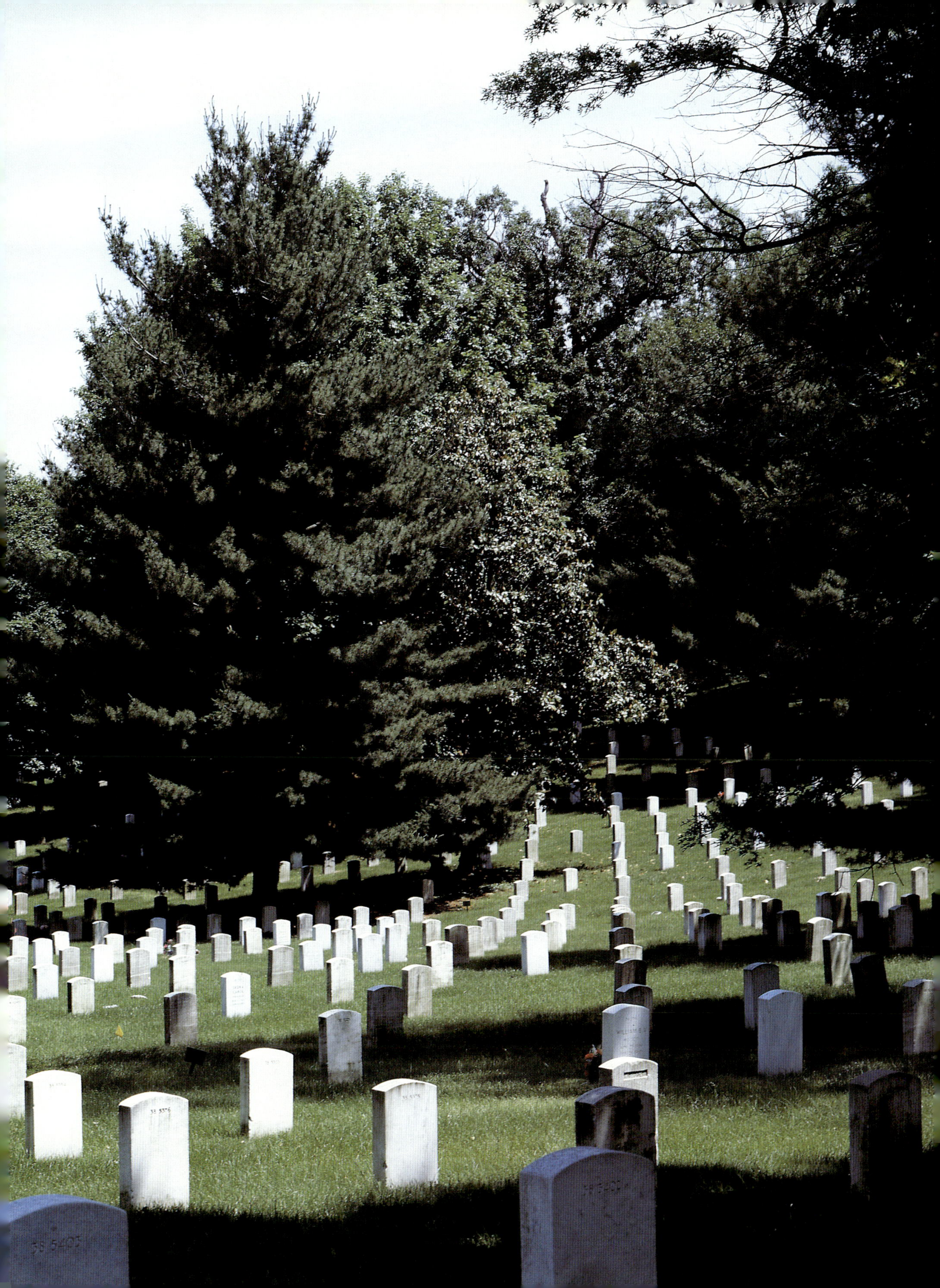

The U.S. Marine Corps War Memorial (right) was sculpted by Felix W. de Weldon, based on news photographer Joe Rosenthal's Pulitzer Prize-winning photo of the flag-raising atop Mount Suribachi on the Pacific island of Iwo Jima after the bloody victory over entrenched Japanese forces in 1945. At Arlington National Cemetery, the gravesites of John F. Kennedy and Jacqueline Kennedy Onassis (opposite) are attended by an eternal flame. Nearby, a cross marks the grave of the president's brother, Robert.

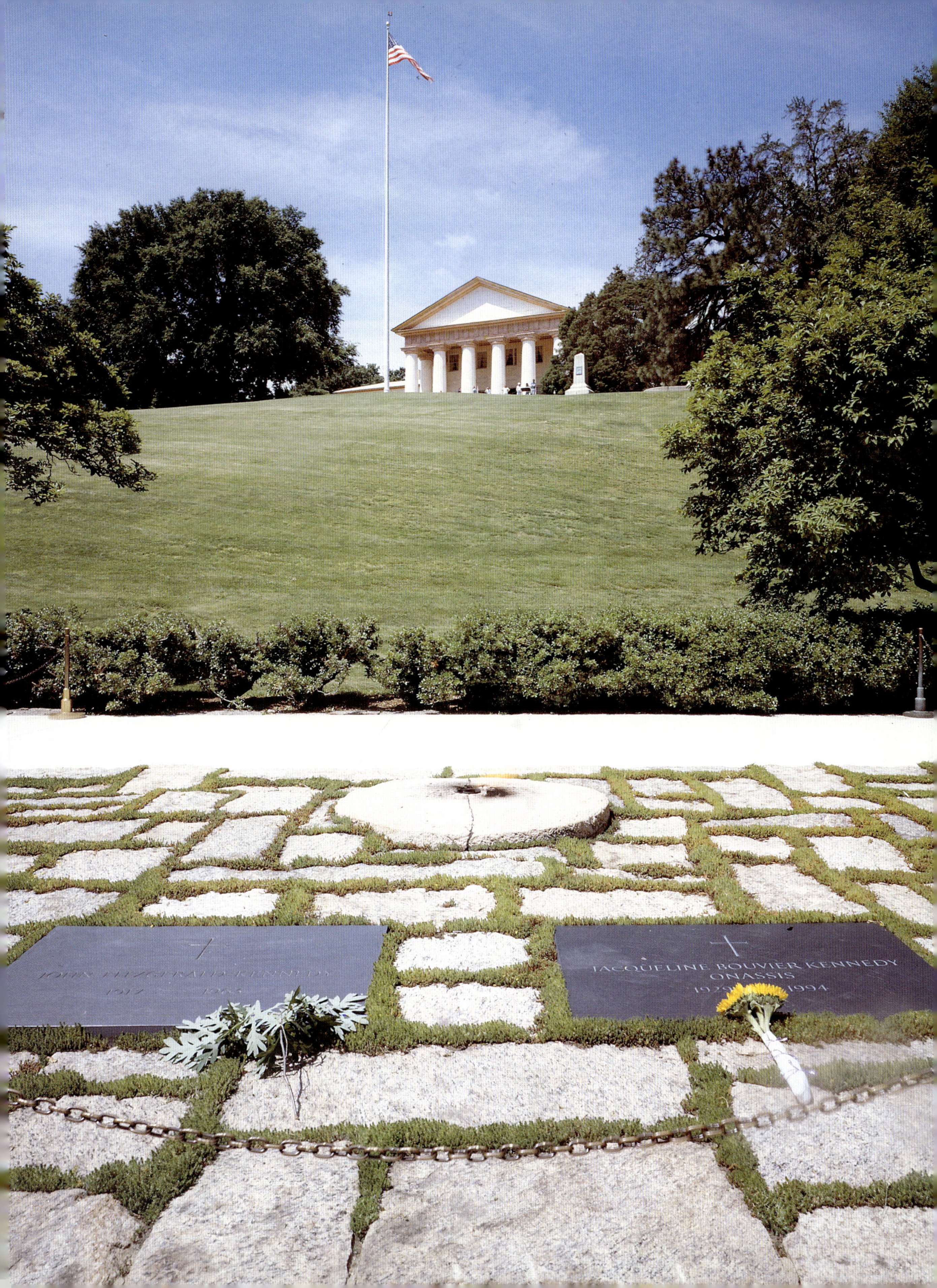
JACQUELINE BOUVIER KENNEDY
ONASSIS

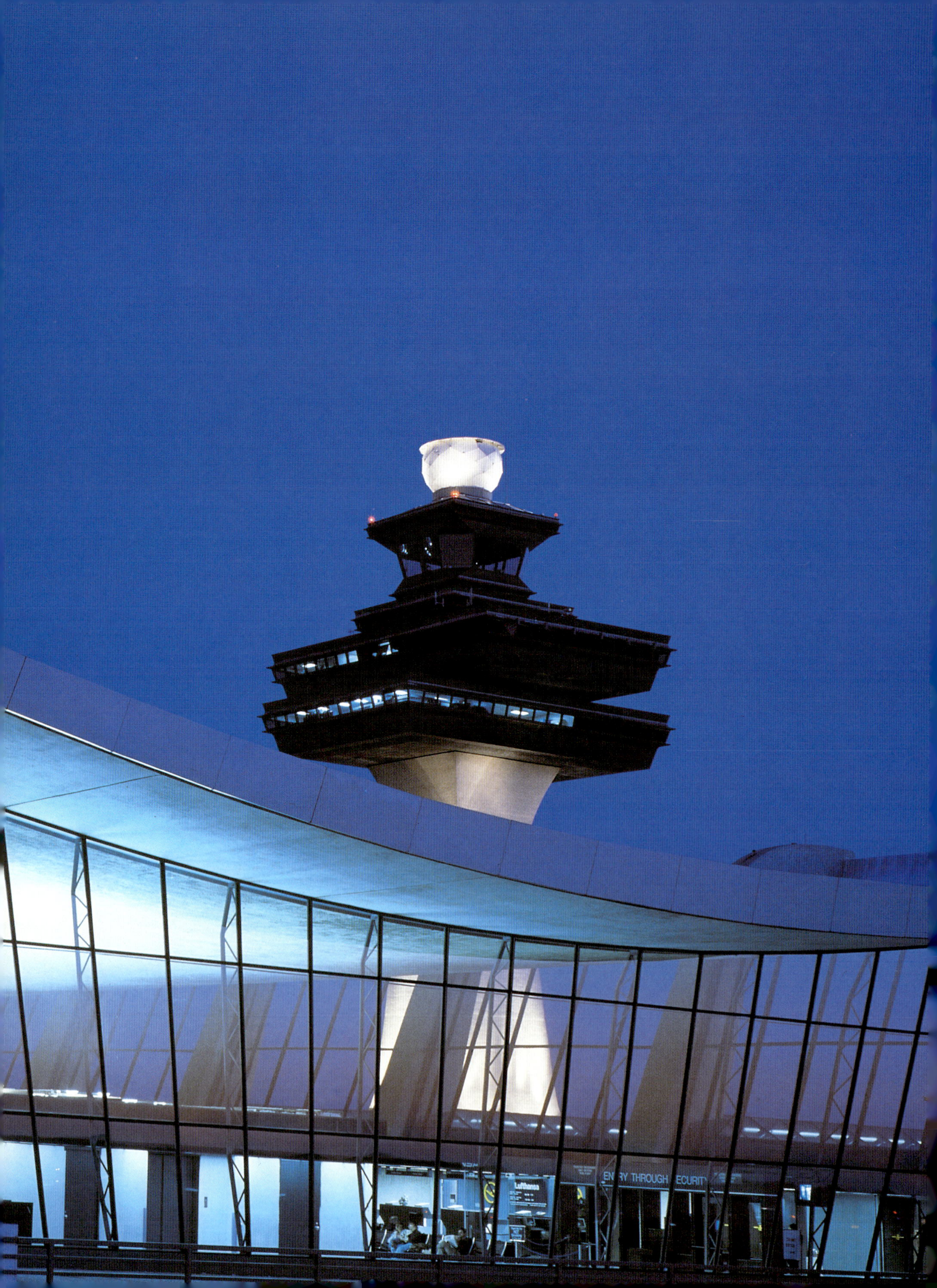

Lufthansa
THROUGH

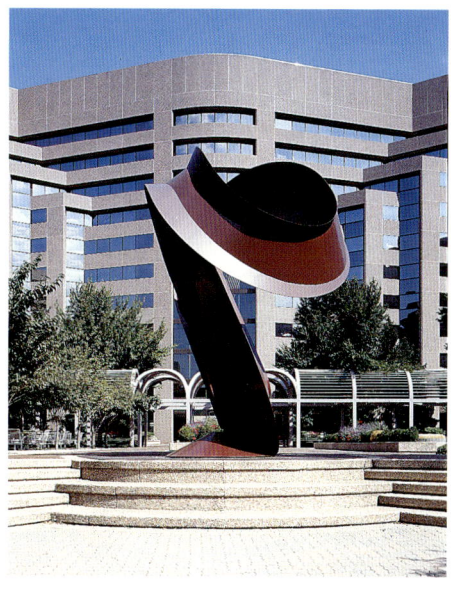

Crystal City (above) is a vast residential, office, and underground retail development along old U.S. Route 1 near the old Washington National Airport, which sprawls over landfill in Virginia, across the Potomac River from the federal city. Rather than create vapid stone and glass caverns, Crystal City's developer, the Charles E. Smith Company, spiced the terrain with extensive landscaping and a variety of public art. Dulles International Airport, named for Secretary of State John Foster Dulles, handled only fifty-three thousand passengers when it opened in farmland straddling Fairfax and Loudoun counties in 1962. Today, thirteen million passengers a year take off on its five runways. Architect Eero Saarinen designed the futuristic concourse (left).

47

Three times a week from September through March, after the sounding of the hunting horn, from twenty to one hundred "members of the field" (above) loose their hounds on any fox who happens to be skulking in the fields near The Plains, west of Manassas. This area of Northern Virginia is horse country. At Locust Hill farm near Middleburg (opposite), thoroughbreds are trained, groomed, and stalled. The big Luck Stone Corporation, founded in 1923, has quarries throughout Virginia. This facility—230 feet deep in spots—in Fairfax County near Manassas Battlefield, harvests graystone and an igneous rock called diabase (overleaf). Many quarries first provided ballast for railroads. Luck's operations supply granite for buildings, rock chips for highways, crushed limestone for farmers, and sand for concrete. Its quarries are converted into lakes or other recreation areas.

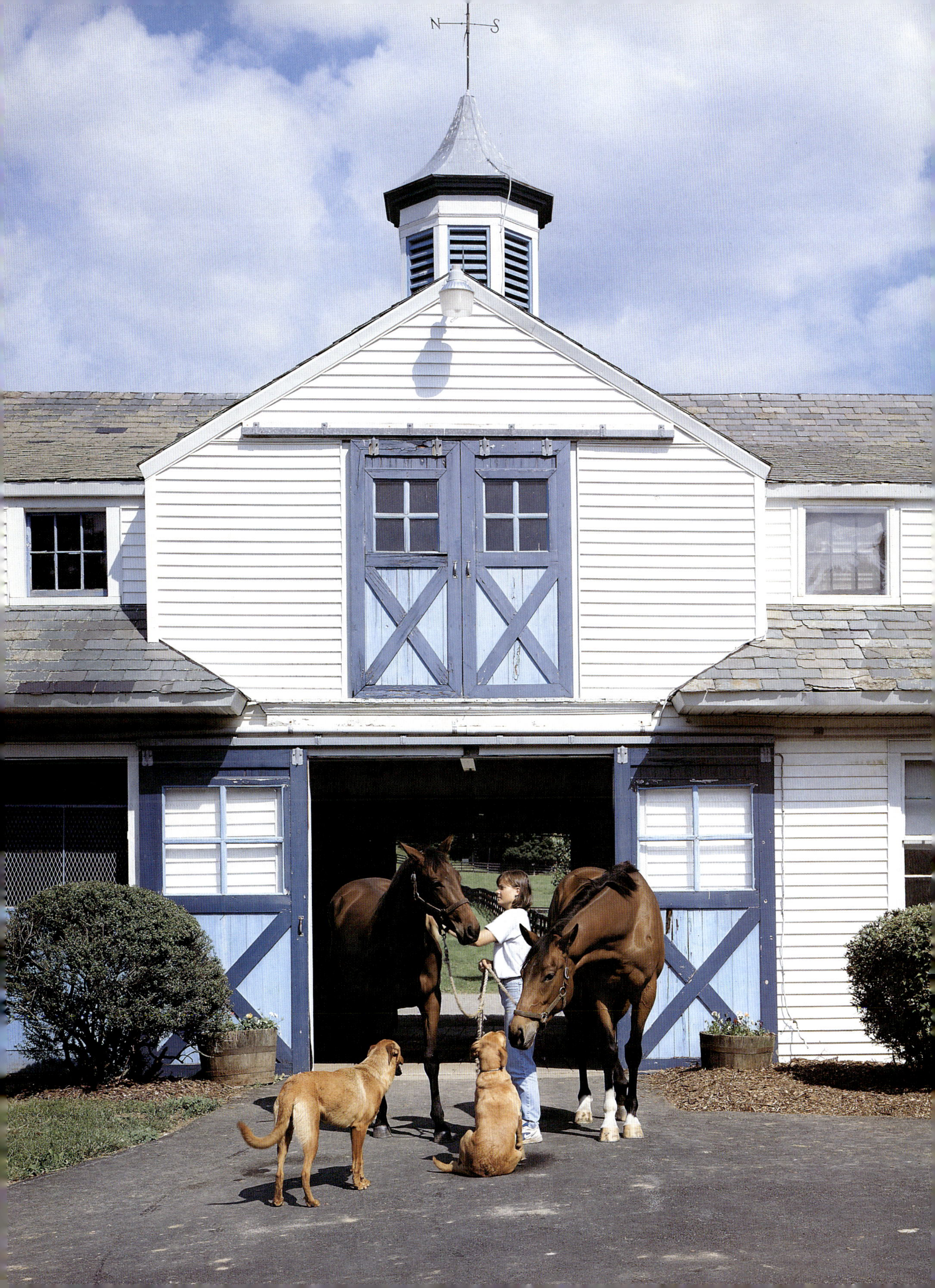
N
S

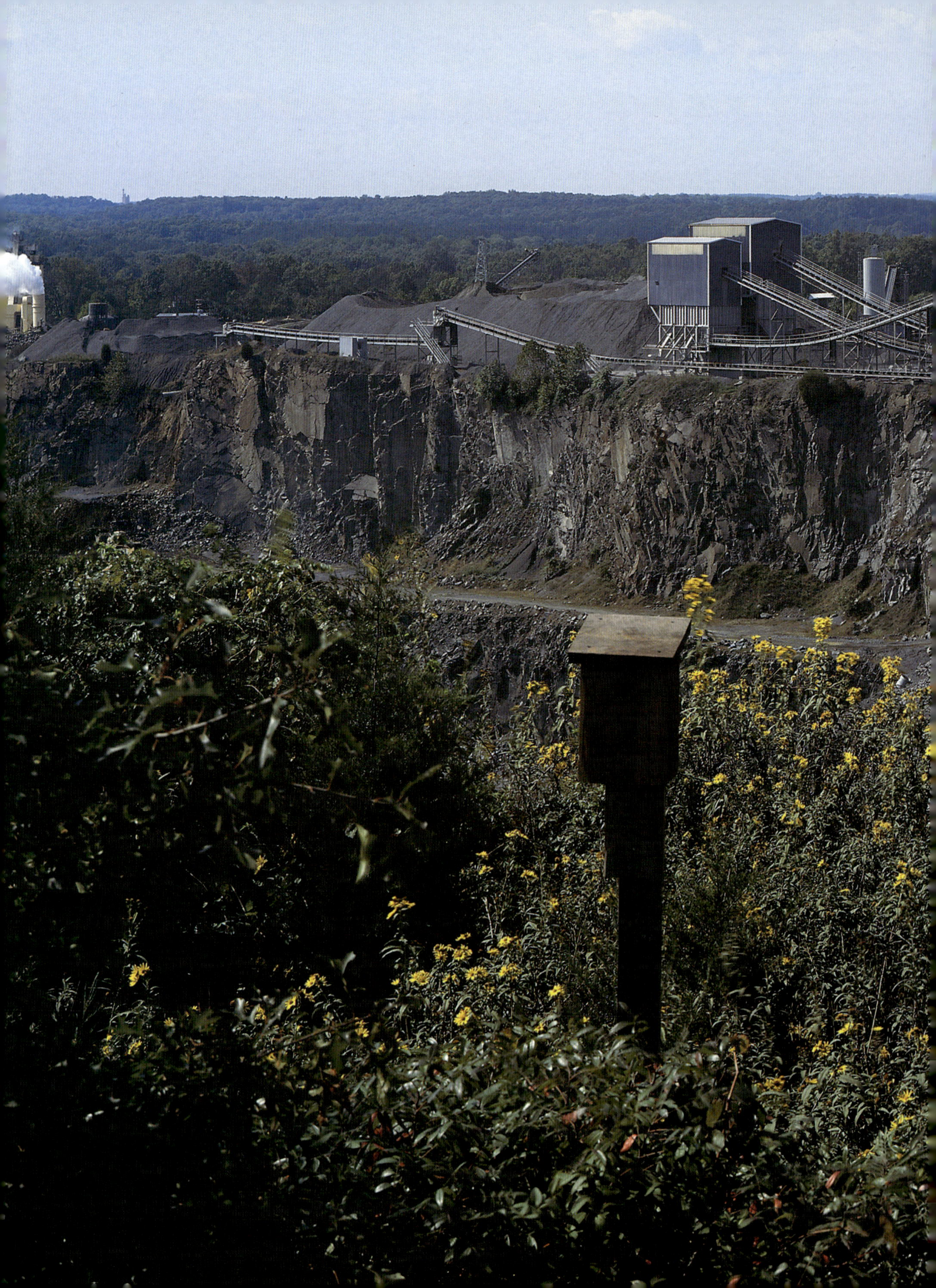

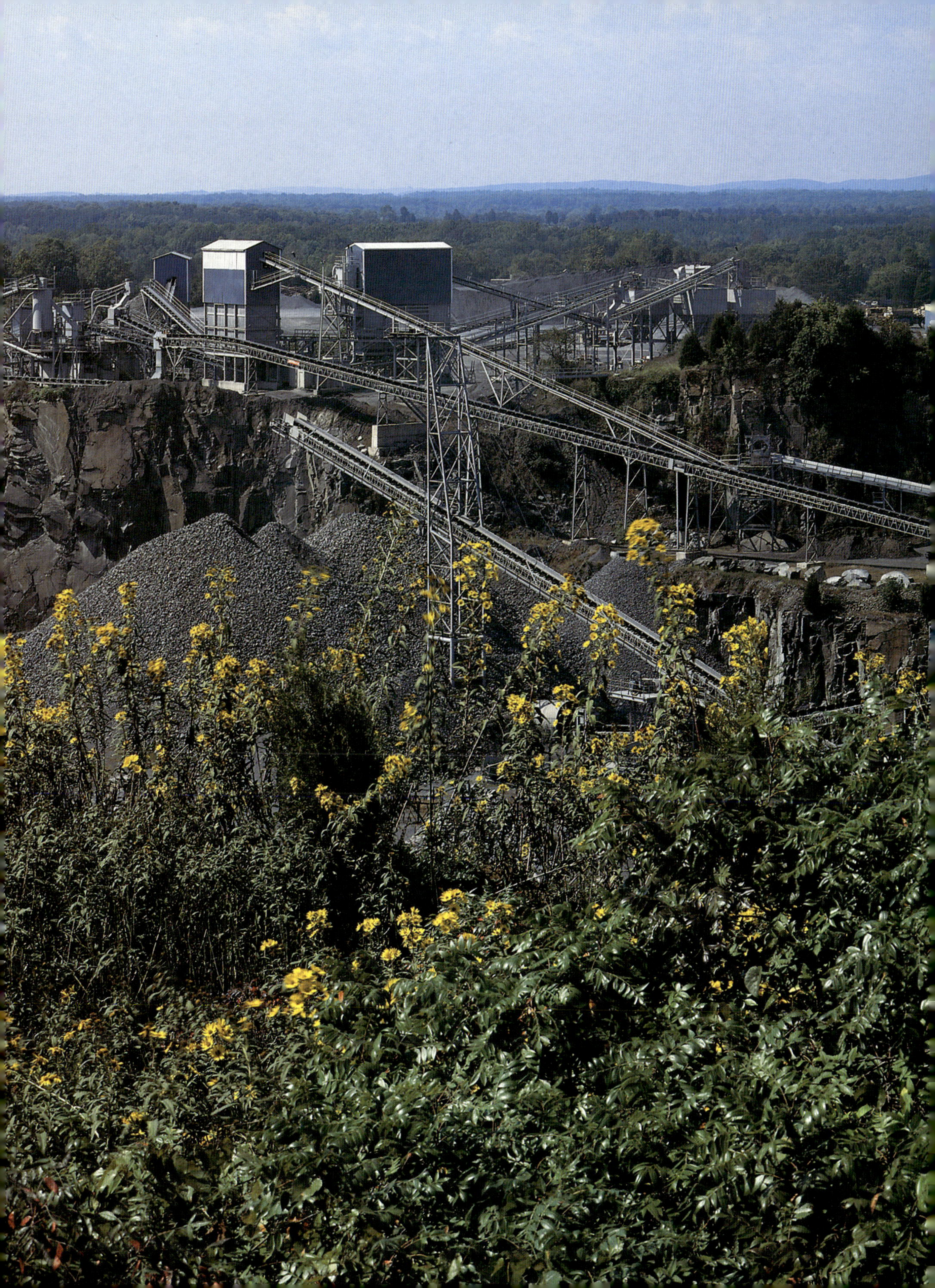

JACKSON
1824-1863

Thomas Jonathan Jackson was a professor of military tactics at Virginia Military Institute in Lexington when he resigned from the U.S. Army to fight for secessionist Virginia. He earned the nickname "Stonewall" while resisting a Union attack at the first Battle of Bull Run. The general is buried in Stonewall Jackson Memorial Cemetery (opposite) in Lexington. At VMI today, cadets still march in crisp formation (top left). Edward Valentine carved the recumbent statue of Robert E. Lee (bottom left) at the chapel of Lexington's Washington and Lee University, where Lee spent his final years as president. He is buried in a family crypt on a lower level. Lee often rode his beloved horse, *Traveller*, into the Shenandoah Valley (overleaf) to meditate.

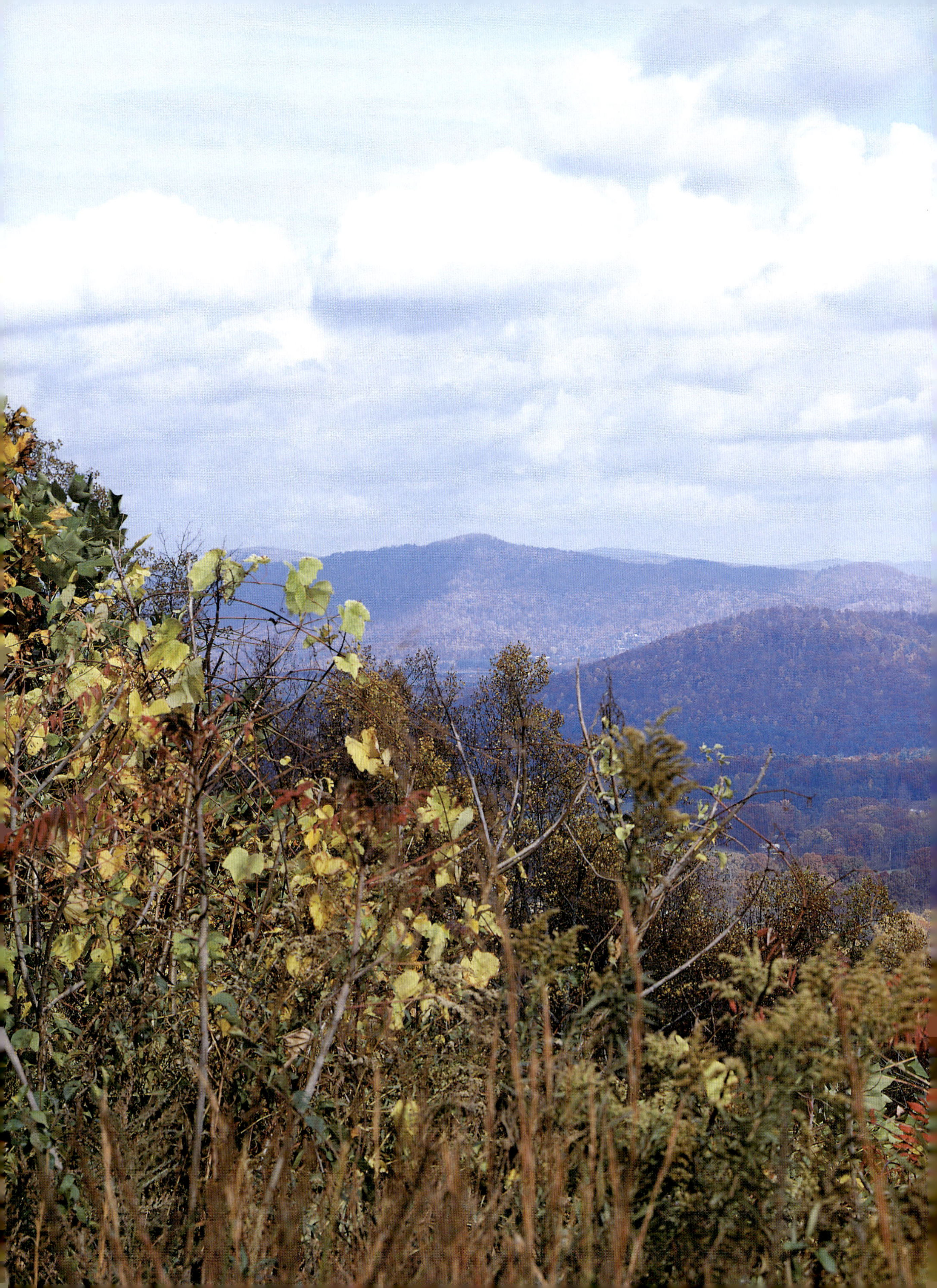

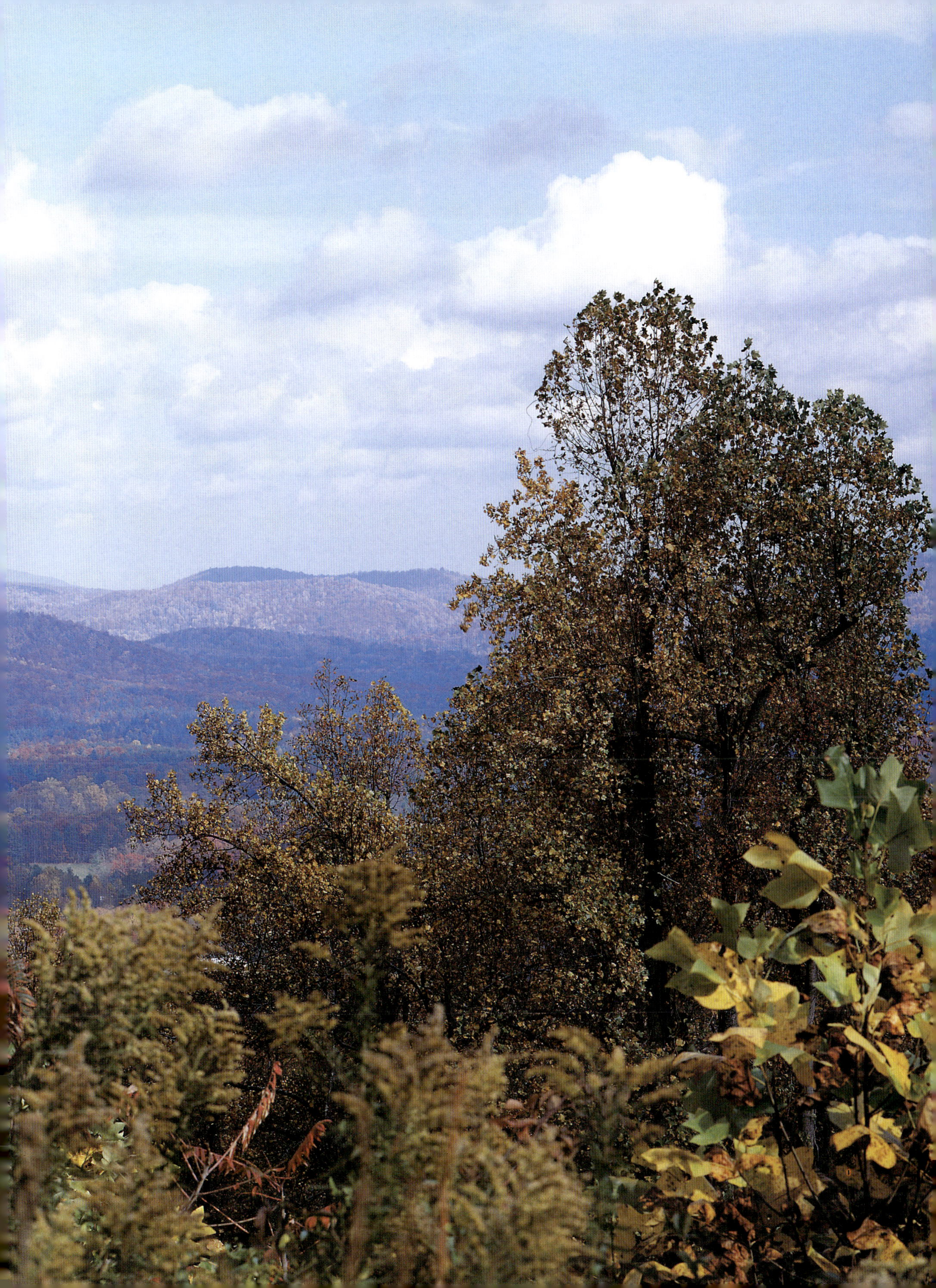

In 1774, King George III granted the incredible Natural Bridge (opposite) to Thomas Jefferson, who surveyed and mapped the area (as had George Washington before him). In 1803, two years after he was inaugurated president, Jefferson built a cabin at the site and invited the first American visitors. The Cedar Creek branch of the James River, in the Shenandoah Valley, formed the rock bridge as it carved a two-hundred-foot gorge. Nearby on the property, spring-fed waters of another creek tumble over a series of waterfalls (right). Next to the attraction's visitor's center is a wax museum featuring figures from Virginia and U.S. history—including (above) Jefferson and John Adams signing the Declaration of Independence.

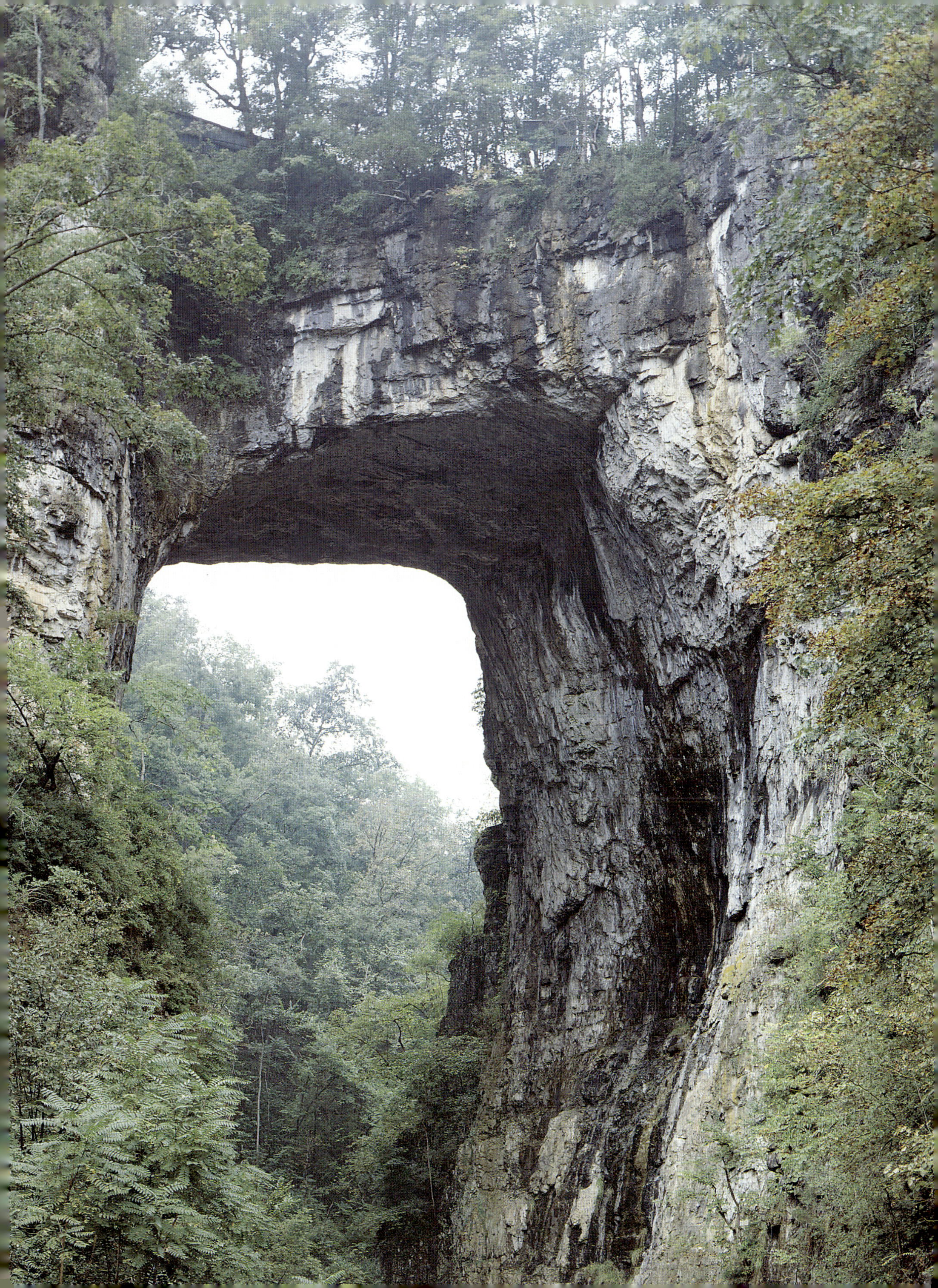

Roanoke, the "Capital of the Blue Ridge," was once Big Lick, a key railroad town. It is also called the "Star City of the South" because of the one-hundred-foot neon star (above) erected on Mill Mountain's overlook in 1949. The platform offers a spectacular view of the Roanoke River Valley (right). Once economically depressed, clean, green Roanoke has rebounded in a big way. A walking tour takes visitors to science and art museums, coffee shops, boutiques and antique galleries, and historic fire and train stations. Roanoke is Virginia's most enthusiastic festival city. Everything from valley strawberries and dogwoods to chili recipes from across the state are celebrated annually.

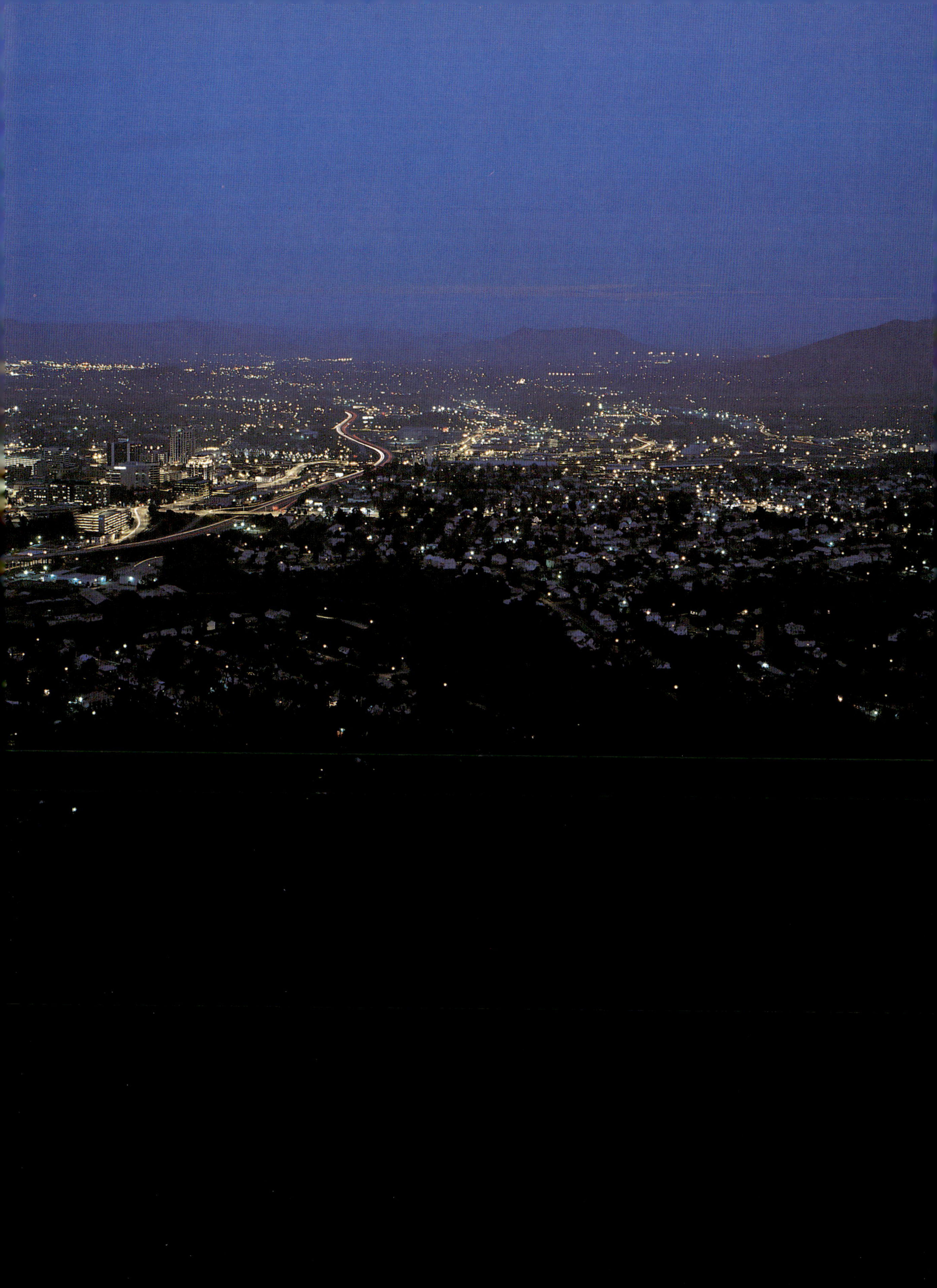

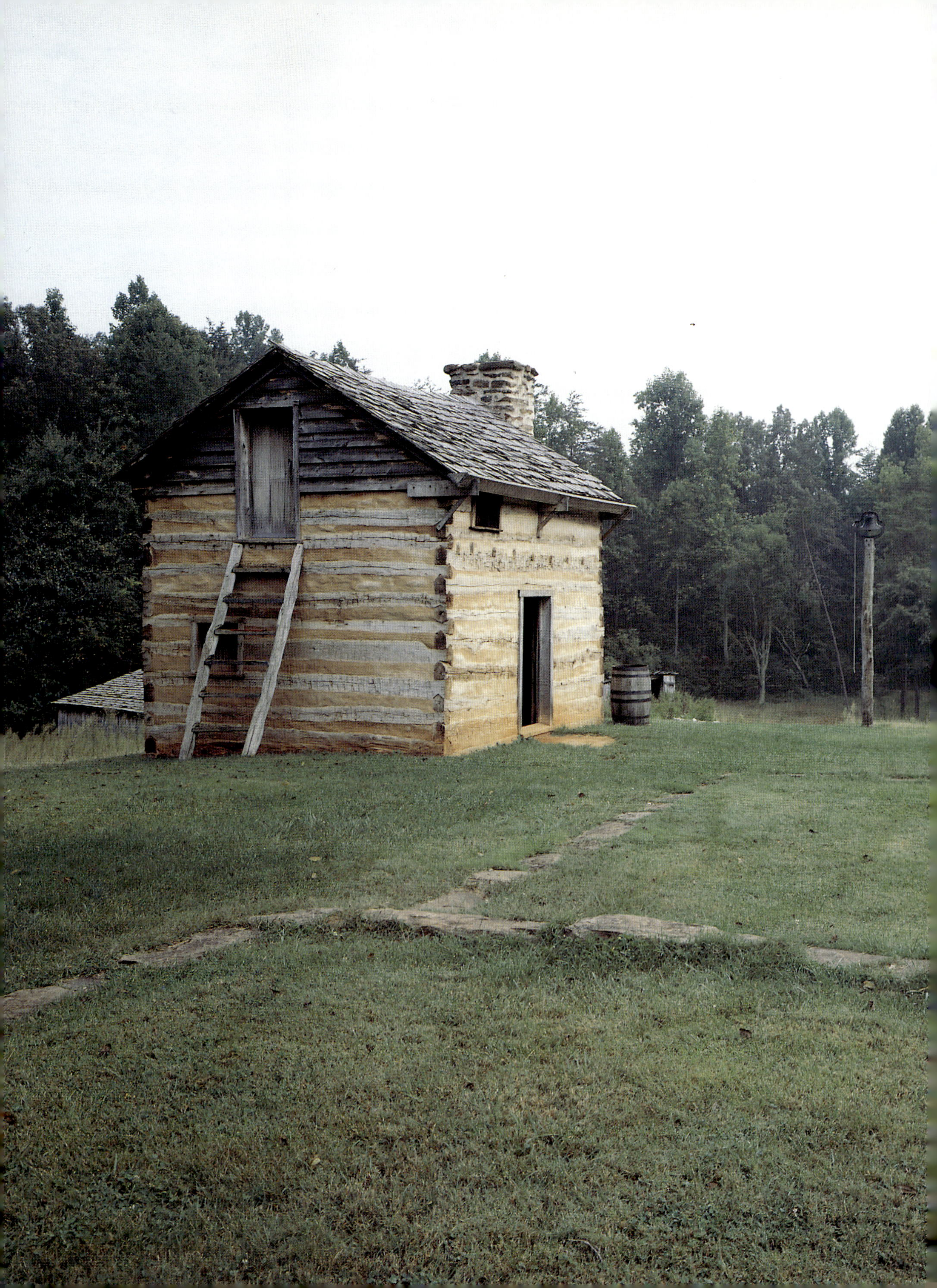

The Booker T. Washington National Monument (left and above), southeast of Roanoke, commemorates the life and accomplishments of Booker Taliferro Washington, born a slave on this Burroughs tobacco farm in 1856. Washington left, uneducated and newly freed, at age nine. He returned for a visit in 1908 as a college president and influential statesman. Washington was an internationally recognized educator, author, and spokesman for his race. He recalled his childhood at this modest farm in his autobiography, Up From Slavery. "There was no period of my life that was devoted to play," he once wrote. His critics charged that his conservative approach to racial harmony actually delayed its quest.

The scenic, 469-mile, toll-free Blue Ridge Parkway stretches from Shenandoah National Park in Virginia through western North Carolina to Great Smoky Mountains National Park in Tennessee. At points such as the Metz Run Overlook (above), the road twists and turns along the crest of the southern Appalachians. Near Buffalo Mountain at mile marker 176 on the parkway, east of Pulaski, Mabry Mill (opposite) is an example of the water-powered gristmills once found on nearly every mountain stream. Blacksmith Ed Mabry built the mill in 1910 and operated it into the 1930s. At this working mill, visitors can watch a miller grind corn into grits, and wheat and buckwheat into flour, as the waters from the millrace turn the large wooden water wheel.

Titles available in the Pictorial Souvenir series

BOSTON

CHICAGO

COLORADO

FLORIDA

MANHATTAN

NEW ENGLAND

NEW ORLEANS

NEW YORK CITY: THE FIVE BOROUGHS

PHILADELPHIA

SAN FRANCISCO

TEXAS

VIRGINIA

WASHINGTON, D.C.